Strike It Rich In Cripple Creek

Leni Donlan

Raintree

Chicago, Illinois

Designed by Michelle Lisseter, Kim Miracle
and Bigtop
Printed in China

11 10 09 08 07
10 9 8 7 6 5 4 3 2 1

**Library of Congress
Cataloging-in-Publication Data**
Donlan, Leni.
   Strike it rich in Cripple Creek : gold rush / Leni
Donlan.
      p. cm. -- (American history through primary
sources)
   Includes bibliographical references and index.
   ISBN 1-4109-2419-X (hc : alk. paper) -- ISBN 1-4109-
2430-0 (pb : alk.
paper)
  1. Cripple Creek Region (Colo.)--Gold discoveries--
Sources--Juvenile
literature. 2. Cripple Creek Region (Colo.)--History--
19th
century--Sources--Juvenile literature. 3. Colorado--
Gold
discoveries--Sources--Juvenile literature. 4. Colorado--
History--To
1876--Sources--Juvenile literature. 5. Frontier and
pioneer life--Cripple
Creek Region (Colo.)--Sources--Juvenile literature. 6.
Gold mines and
mining--Cripple Creek Region (Colo.)--History--19th
century--Sources--Juvenile literature. I. Title. II.
Series.
F784.C8D66 2007
978.8'58--dc22

                                        2006004008

13-digit ISBNs
978-1-4109-2419-3 (hardcover)
978-1-4109-2430-8 (paperback)

Acknowledgments
The author and publisher are grateful to the
following for permission to reproduce copyright
material: Denver Public Library, Western History
Collection **pp. 5** (McClure, MCC-2869), **7** (Kemp,
K-8), **8** (McClure, MCC-1918), **9** (X-61053), **12–13**
(X-21803), **14–15** (X-60244), **16–17** (X-811), **18–19**
(X-21830), **20–21** (X-22176), **22–23** (D.P. Morgan,
X-61139), **24–25** (Poley, P-817), **26–27** (J.G. Wilson,
X-809); Gates/Getty Images **p. 4**; Library of Congress
Geography and Map Division **p. 10**; Library of
Congress Prints and Photographs Division **pp. 6, 11**.

Cover photograph of a miner panning for gold
reproduced with permission of Denver Public Library,
Western History Collection (MCC-1918).

Photo research by Tracy Cummins.

Illustrations by Darren Lingard.

The publishers would like to thank Nancy Harris
and Joy Rogers for their assistance in the preparation
of this book.

Every effort has been made to contact copyright
holders of any material reproduced in this book. Any
omissions will be rectified in subsequent printings if
notice is given to the publishers.

Disclaimer
All the Internet addresses (URLs) given in this book
were valid at the time of going to press. However, due
to the dynamic nature of the Internet, some addresses
may have changed, or sites may have changed or
ceased to exist since publication. While the author and
publishers regret any inconvenience this may cause
readers, no responsibility for any such changes can be
accepted by either the author or the publishers.

It is recommended that adults supervise children on
the Internet.

Contents

Some words are printed in bold, **like this**. You can find out what they mean on page 30. You can also look in the box at the bottom of the page where they first appear.

Gold Fever

Gold is a symbol (sign) of riches and treasure. It is a soft, yellow material. It is found in the earth.

Gold does not **tarnish** (lose its color). Gold does not **corrode** (wear away). Gold can be shaped into beautiful jewelry and other art.

Gold is not only beautiful. It can also be used in many ways. Gold can be used to make electronic equipment. It is used to make computers.

Many people rush to places where gold is found. They dream of finding gold. They dream of getting rich fast!

People like to wear ▶ gold jewelry because of its beauty.

corrode   wear away
tarnish   become dull or discolored

5

Some people say the wish to find gold is like a burning fever. "Gold fever" can make people behave in strange ways. People with gold fever might sell their home. They might quit their jobs. They might move to an area where gold has been found.

Rushing for Gold

Starting in the mid-1800s, Americans rushed to the West. They were looking for gold. For more than 50 years, Americans had gold fever.

Gold fever made people rush to places where gold had been found. This movement was called a **gold rush**. There were many gold rushes.

▼ *This picture shows San Francisco in 1850.*

Gold rush city

San Francisco in California was at the center of the California gold rush. Many people came to San Francisco during the gold rush years. By 1849 more than 100,000 people were living there.

Very few people struck it rich in any gold rush. Still, gold rushes changed the United States forever. Cities and towns developed where gold was found.

When a gold rush ended, some towns became empty. These towns are known as **ghost towns**. Other towns and cities continued to grow after a gold rush ended. They have become major cities we still know today.

▼ This is a ghost town. It is all that is left of Ashcroft, Colorado. Ashcroft was a busy town in the 1880s.

7

ghost town   town that people have left empty
gold rush   when many people rush to a place where gold has been discovered

Taking Gold from the Earth

Prospectors are people who look for gold. Prospectors sometimes find gold in or near a stream. They scoop sand and gravel from the stream into pans. This is called **panning** for gold. They wash the sand and gravel out of the pan. If they are lucky, they will find gold left behind.

This miner is ▶
hoping to find
some gold!

miner	person who works in a mine (an underground tunnel)
pan	item used to scoop sand and gravel from a stream
prospector	person who looks for gold and other valuable natural substances
sluice	using a box and flowing water to separate gold from mud and sand

▲ *In the 1800s miners used candles to light their work area.*

Sluicing is another way prospectors get gold. They shovel mud, sand, and pebbles from the bottom of streams into long boxes. Then water is run through the boxes. The mud and sand are washed away. If they are lucky, the prospectors find the heavier gold left behind.

Miners are prospectors, too. They work in mines (tunnels underground). They dig or blast tunnels to find gold in rock.

49ers and 59ers

49ers

The first big **gold rush** started in 1849. It began after people found gold in California. More than 60,000 **prospectors** came to California. They came from all over the world. They were looking for gold. These prospectors were named "49ers" after the 1849 gold rush.

This is a map of ▶
California in 1851.

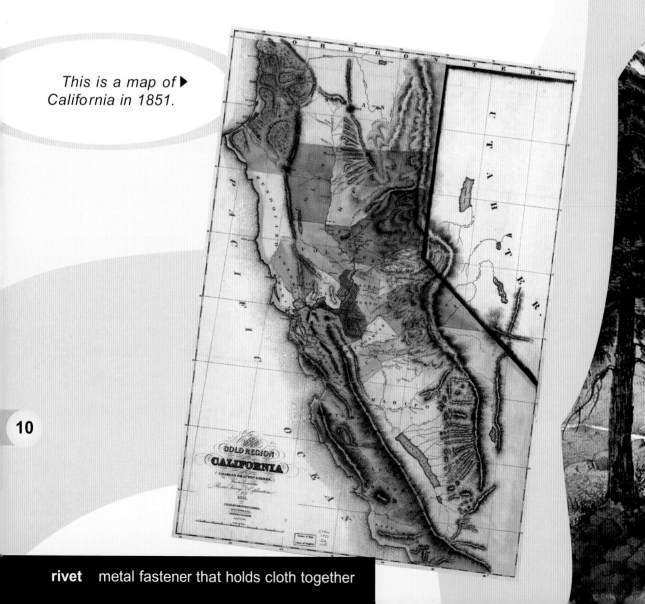

rivet   metal fastener that holds cloth together

Levi Strauss started a business during this gold rush. He made blue denim (blue jean) pants. He made them for prospectors. He added **rivets** to the pockets. Rivets are metal fasteners. This made the pants very strong.

Blue jeans

The Levi Strauss company is still making blue jeans. They make jeans for men, women, and children. Levi's blue jeans are sold in more than 100 countries.

▼ *These prospectors are looking for gold in a stream.*

59ers

Another **gold rush** began in 1859. This started after gold was found in the area that is now Colorado. Many people moved to Colorado to find gold. These **prospectors** were called "59ers."

The lettering on these▼ prospectors' wagon reads: "Pikes Peak or Bust 1860."

The prospectors moved to the Colorado mountains. Pikes Peak is one of the tallest mountains in Colorado. It was a famous **landmark** (marker) for travelers during the gold rush.

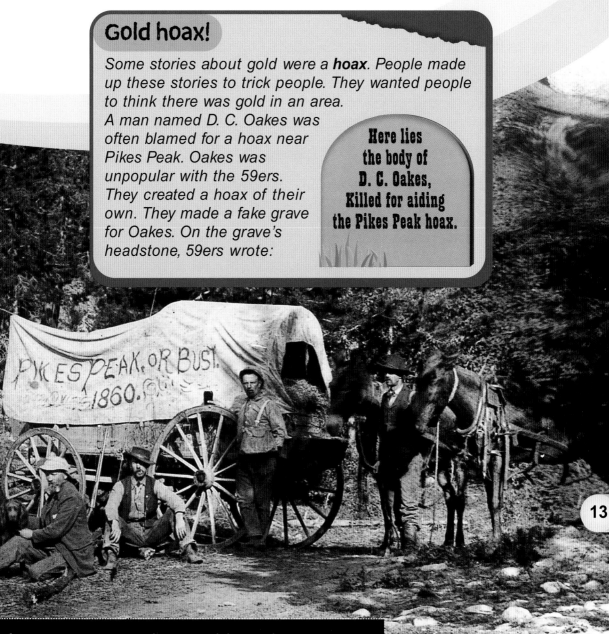

Gold hoax!

*Some stories about gold were a **hoax**. People made up these stories to trick people. They wanted people to think there was gold in an area. A man named D. C. Oakes was often blamed for a hoax near Pikes Peak. Oakes was unpopular with the 59ers. They created a hoax of their own. They made a fake grave for Oakes. On the grave's headstone, 59ers wrote:*

Here lies
the body of
D. C. Oakes,
Killed for aiding
the Pikes Peak hoax.

hoax   story made up to trick people
landmark   something that marks a certain place

Cripple Creek, Colorado

In 1884 there was another gold **hoax** (trick). It was about Pikes Peak.

A man nicknamed "Chicken Bill" thought up this hoax. Bill put some gold in an area near Cripple Creek, Colorado. Then he filed a **claim**. People file claims so they can own the land where they found gold. Then they will own all the gold found there in the future.

Thousands of gold **prospectors** rushed to the area. They thought they could find claims, too. They soon found out that Chicken Bill's claim was a hoax. He hadn't really found gold. He had just put some gold there himself. The prospectors were angry with Chicken Bill. He was almost hanged.

For years after this hoax, most prospectors stayed away from the Cripple Creek area. The **gold rush** crowds disappeared.

14

claim   process that makes people own
        the land where they found gold

▲ These men are using a gold pan, pick, and shovel to look for gold in Colorado.

Welty and Womack

Levi Welty was a **gold prospector** who stayed in Colorado. He didn't find gold. Still, Welty decided to stay in the area. He and his family started a cattle ranch. A story is told about how Welty named Cripple Creek. It goes like this:

One day, Welty and his sons were working along a creek (stream). A log fell and hurt Welty's son. Then, Welty shot himself by mistake. He injured himself. The shotgun blast scared some cattle. A scared calf started running. It tried to jump over the creek . It broke its leg. Welty said to his sons, "This sure is some cripple creek!"

Bob Womack stayed in the area, too. Womack and his brother bought the Cripple Creek Ranch from Levi Welty. The year was 1876.

Gold fever kept Womack in Cripple Creek. He said there was gold to be found. No one believed him. But they should have listened to Womack!

▲ This cabin cost the Womacks $500 and two pigs.

The Last Great Colorado Gold Rush

In 1890 Bob Womack finally found some gold. He dug **shafts** in the ground. Shafts are long, narrow tunnels. Bob used a pick and a shovel. He dug and dug.

After months of digging, Womack found hard rock. The rock showed some **veins**. Veins are lines in rock. They are a different color from the rest of the rock. The color of the veins can show if there is gold in the rock.

Womack exploded the rock. He used dynamite. To his great joy, he found chunks of GOLD! Womack never became a rich man, though.

People heard about Womack's discovery. They got interested in Cripple Creek again. Gold **prospectors** began arriving. Another **gold rush** was on!

▼ *The Palace Hotel in Cripple Creek was very busy during the gold rush.*

shaft long, narrow tunnel into the earth

vein line in rock that is a different color from the rest of the rock

Striking It Rich

Winfield S. Stratton became very rich from Cripple Creek gold. Stratton first came to Colorado in 1868. He worked as a carpenter. He stayed in Colorado. He believed he would find gold. It took him more than twenty years to do so!

Finally, Stratton made a gold **claim**. A claim allows people to own the land where they found gold. Stratton made his claim on July 4, 1891.

Stratton had **mines** on this land. Mines are tunnels under the earth. **Miners** work in mines. They collect and remove gold. Stratton's mines earned him millions of dollars. He was an important person in Cripple Creek history.

mine   tunnel under the surface of the earth

▼ This is a portrait of Winfield S. Stratton.

Mining Pays in Cripple Creek

By 1891 many gold **prospectors** moved to Cripple Creek. They lived in tents and cabins. Cripple Creek was soon home to almost 5,000 people.

Prospectors **panned** for gold in the streams of Cripple Creek. They used a pan to scoop mud and sand from the bottom of a stream. They hoped they would find gold in their pans. Some people found a little gold this way.

The prospectors used ▶ burros (donkeys) like these to help carry their supplies.

The largest amounts of gold were found in **mines**. The mines were deep tunnels in the earth. The most money was made from mining gold. The deeper down the mines went, the more gold the **miners** found.

The early mines took gold worth $250,000 from the earth. By the time the gold rush ended, mining in Cripple Creek had earned over $400 million.

Problems in Cripple Creek

The **miners** were not always paid the same. Some miners had to work longer hours than others. The miners wanted to be treated fairly.

The miners **organized** themselves into a group. The group became a **labor union**. This labor union worked to improve their pay. It worked to improve their working conditions.

The labor union in Cripple Creek called a **strike**. In a strike, workers stop working. They start working again when the owners and the labor union agree. They must agree on what is fair.

Cripple Creek had another big problem. On April 25 and 29, 1896, fires burned in Cripple Creek. Thousands of people lost their homes. Much of the city was destroyed. Within six months, the city was rebuilt. It was bigger and busier than ever!

labor union	group of workers who agree to act together
organized	working together as a team
strike	when a group of workers stops working

▲ *This is a picture of the Palace Hotel. It was taken after the second Cripple Creek fire in 1896.*

Life in Cripple Creek

During the **gold rush**, Cripple Creek was an exciting place to be. There were dance halls and hotels. There were businesses of all kinds.

Families and single gold **prospectors** lived in the area. Most people lived in unpainted **shacks**. Shacks are small, cheaply-built houses. These shacks did not have indoor plumbing. People had outdoor toilets called outhouses.

The whole city celebrated holidays together. But the people of Cripple Creek did not always get along together. There were many gunfights and robberies in Cripple Creek.

Today, Cripple Creek is a quieter place. It has become a popular vacation spot. Visitors enjoy tours and museums.

Busy city

*By 1893 Cripple Creek had four dance halls, seven bakeries, nine hotels, ten meat markets, eleven clothing stores, twenty-four grocery stores, six bookstores, twenty-six **saloons**, and at least forty-eight lawyers!*

saloon   place where alcohol is served
shack   small, cheaply-built house

27

Gold Rush Cities

Dreams of gold took people to the following areas.

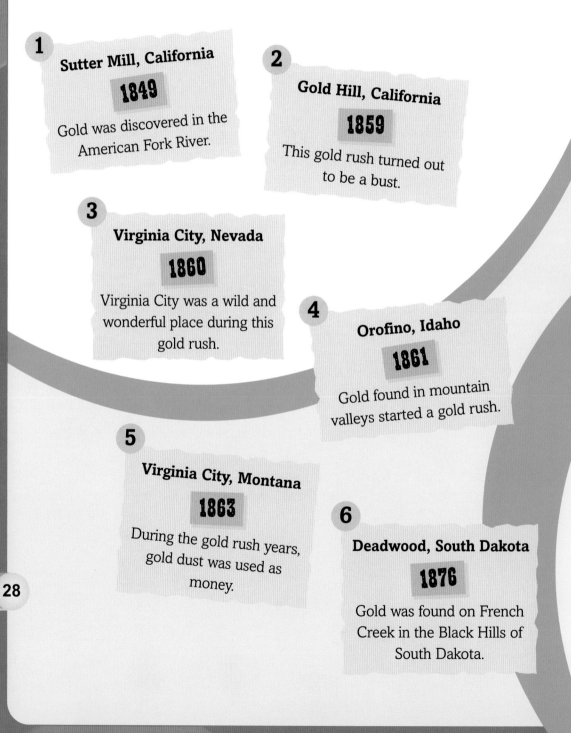

1 Sutter Mill, California

1849

Gold was discovered in the American Fork River.

2 Gold Hill, California

1859

This gold rush turned out to be a bust.

3 Virginia City, Nevada

1860

Virginia City was a wild and wonderful place during this gold rush.

4 Orofino, Idaho

1861

Gold found in mountain valleys started a gold rush.

5 Virginia City, Montana

1863

During the gold rush years, gold dust was used as money.

6 Deadwood, South Dakota

1876

Gold was found on French Creek in the Black Hills of South Dakota.

28

8

Cripple Creek, Colorado

1892

Another gold rush began high in Colorado's Rocky Mountains.

7

Tombstone, Arizona

1877

Not much gold, but silver was discovered near Tombstone.

9

Nome, Alaska

1899

Gold was found on the beach of the Bering Sea in Nome, Alaska.

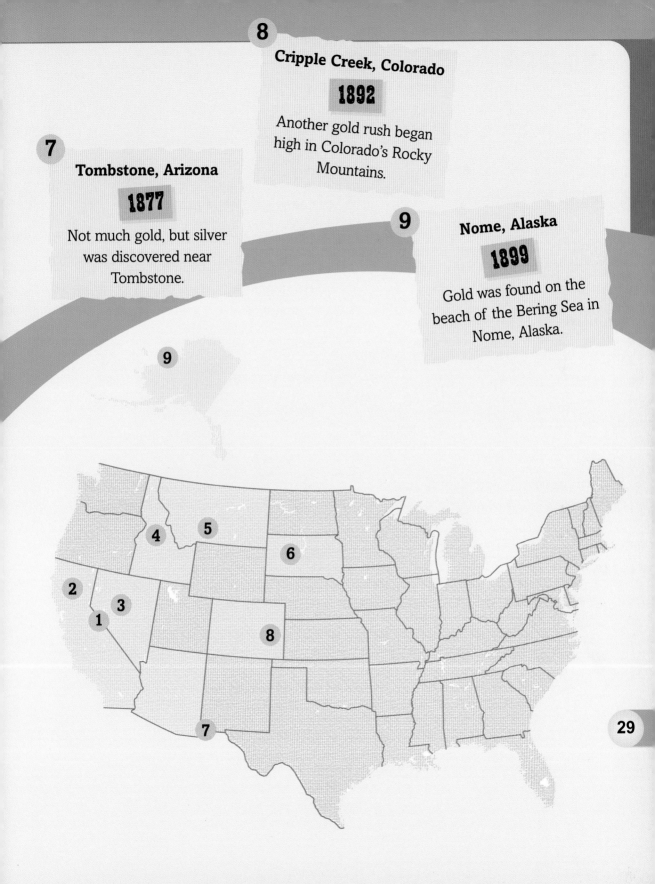

Glossary

claim process that makes people own the land where they found gold

corrode wear away

ghost town town that people have left empty

gold rush when many people rush to a place where gold has been discovered

herd group of animals

hoax story made up to trick people

labor union group of workers who agree to act together. They try to improve their pay and working conditions.

landmark something that marks a certain place. Landmarks help people know where they are.

mine tunnel under the surface of the earth. In a mine, natural substances such as gold and coal are taken from the earth.

miner person who works in a mine. A mine is an underground tunnel.

organized working together as a team

pan using a pan to scoop sand and gravel from a stream. Then, you wash away the sand and gravel to see if any gold remains.

prospector person who looks for gold and other valuable natural substances

rivet metal fastener that holds cloth together

saloon place where alcohol is served

shack small, cheaply-built house

shaft long, narrow tunnel into the earth. Shafts are used in mines to find substances such as gold.

sluice using a box and flowing water to separate valuable gold from worthless material, such as sand

strike when a group of workers stops working. They strike to protest against low pay or bad working conditions.

tarnish become dull or discolored

vein line in rock that is a different color from the rest of the rock

Want to Know More?

Books to read

- Kalman, Bobbie, and Kate Calder. *The Life of a Miner*. New York: Crabtree, 2000.
- Murphy, Claire Rudolf, and Jane G. Haigh. *Children of the Gold Rush*. Portland, OR: Alaska Northwest, 2001.
- Schanzer, Rosalyn. *Gold Fever!* New York: Scholastic, 2000.

Websites

- http://www.cripple-creek.org
  Find pictures and information about Cripple Creek at the Cripple Creek District Museum's site.
- http://www.museumca.org/goldrush
  Read about gold fever, 49ers, the gold rush, and much more at this site.
- http://www.isu.edu/~trinmich/funfacts.html
  Read fun facts about the gold rush at this site.

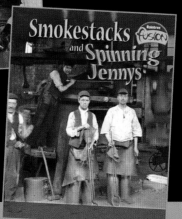

Read **Tenement Stories: Immigrant Life** to find out what life was like for immigrants living in New York in the 1800s.

Read **Smokestacks and Spinning Jennys: Industrial Revolution** to discover how new inventions changed our lives.

31

Index